FANTASTIC FACTS
TREES

PETER MELLETT

southwater

This edition is published by Southwater

Distributed in the UK by
The Manning Partnership
251–253 London Road East
Batheaston
Bath BA1 7RL
UK
tel. (0044) 01225 852 727
fax (0044) 01225 852 852

Distributed in Australia by
Sandstone Publishing
Unit 1, 360 Norton Street
Leichhardt
New South Wales 2040
Australia
tel. (0061) 2 9560 7888
fax (0061) 2 9560 7488

Distributed in New Zealand by
Five Mile Press NZ
PO Box 33-1071
Glenfield
Auckland 10
New Zealand
tel. (0064) 9 4444 144
fax (0064) 9 4444 518

Southwater is an imprint of Anness Publishing Limited
© 1997, 2000 Anness Publishing Limited

1 3 5 7 9 10 8 6 4 2

Publisher: Joanna Lorenz
Editor: Charlotte Evans
Consultant: Michael Chinery
Photographer: Tim Ridley
Stylists: Tim Grabham, Ken Campbell and Marion Elliot
Designer: Caroline Grimshaw
Picture Researcher: Marion Elliot
Illustrator: Alisa Tingley

The Publishers would like to thank the following children, and their
parents, for modelling in this book – Charlene Da Cova, Anthony
Daniels, Laura Harris-Stewart, Lauren Hooper, Mitzi Hooper,
Hollie Victoria Howell, Vadim Khramov, Justyna Kucharska,
Kevin Loke, Nabil Mehdinejad, Tara Minto. They would also
like to thank Duncan Goodwin and Steve Hooper Gardens.

Previously published as *Learn About Trees*

TREES

CONTENTS

4 • Parts of a tree

6 • Measuring a tree

8 • Roots

10 • Pumping water

12 • Trunks and bark

14 • Looking at bark

16 • Needles and leaves

18 • From bud to leaf

20 • Living processes

22 • Light and water

24 • Pollination

26 • From flower to fruit

28 • Fruits and seeds

30 • Scattering seeds

32 • Germination

34 • Conifer forests

36 • Temperate forests

38 • Life in a tree

40 • Tropical trees

42 • Savanna woodland

44 • Swamps

46 • Amazing trees

48 • Leaf fall, death and decay

50 • Life in the leaf litter

52 • Prehistoric trees

54 • Wood as a material

56 • Chemicals from trees

58 • Pollution and destruction

60 • Conservation

62 • Make a tree museum

64 • Index

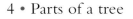

PARTS OF A TREE

TREES are plants that grow all around the world, from the frozen arctic to the steamy jungles around the equator. Wherever they grow and whatever their shape, we find that all trees have three things in common – they all have roots, leaves and a single, woody trunk. The part above the trunk is called the crown and is made up of branches, twigs and leaves. The crown gives each tree its own distinctive shape.

Unlike us, trees grow throughout their lives. Each year a whole new layer grows under their bark, making them a little fatter. At the same time, roots and twigs grow longer, increasing the tree's spread above and below the ground.

FACT BOX

• The roots of a mature oak cover the same area as a football field.

• A tropical balsa tree can grow 6 feet taller in a year, while an arctic Sitka spruce may grow only 1 inch in a year.

• The first trees (*Archaeopteris*) grew over 350 million years ago.

• The Tasmanian huon pines are the oldest known living trees. It is thought that some of these species are at least 10,000 years old.

• The tallest living trees are some eucalyptus trees that are growing in Australia. One of these species was recently measured at over 500 feet tall.

Leaves
Leaves are where the tree makes its food. Green leaves use sunlight to make sugary sap by joining water from the ground with carbon dioxide gas from the air.

Buds
Buds form at the tips of twigs. They also appear along the sides of twigs and thinner branches. Flowers, or new leaves and stems, grow from the buds in spring.

Like all trees, this oak has roots, a trunk, branches, twigs and leaves. It grew from a tiny acorn that sprouted more than 150 years ago. Each year the girth of its trunk will increase by about 1 inch and it will produce up to 50,000 acorns.

Bark

Bark is the woody skin that prevents a tree from drying out. It also protects the tree from attack by animals and fungi. Old bark splits as the tree's branches and trunk grow thicker each year.

Acorn

Root

Branches

The largest branches grow out from the main trunk of the tree. These branches divide into smaller and smaller branches. At the ends of these are twigs from which leaves grow. All branches start life as thin twigs when a tree is young.

Seeds

Acorns are the seeds of an oak tree. They fall to the ground, where some may sprout and become new oak trees. Most acorns rot or are eaten by animals.

Roots

As a seedling develops, its roots grow into the soil. They will support the fully grown tree against the force of the wind. Roots also take in water and nutrients that help the tree grow.

MEASURING A TREE

Bark — Growth ring

You can clearly see the growth rings on the trunk of this old oak tree. Each year the tree grows a new ring of wood just under the bark.

How can we find out how old or how tall a tree is? How wide is its crown of branches and leaves? When a tree is cut down, you can find out how old it is by counting the growth rings on the stump. There will be one ring for each year of its life. If there are 100 rings, then the tree has lived for 100 years. To discover much more about a living tree, you can measure it in different ways. The problem about measuring trees is that they are far too big to measure with a ruler. It is also unsafe to climb to the top of a tree. The only way to measure a tree is indirectly, without touching it. With the help of a friend, these two projects will help you estimate the size of a tree and the width of its crown.

*You will need:
tape measure, yardstick,
felt tip marker,
notebook, pencil.*

Measuring a tree's height

1 With the tape measure, measure 21 feet from the tree and push the stick into the ground. Measure another yard from the stick and lie down straight on the ground.

2 Use one eye to line up the top of the tree with the stick. Mark this point on the yardstick and measure its height from the ground. The tree's height is 20 times this distance.

M A T E R I A L S

You will need: compass, 8 markers, tape measure, notebook, pencil, graph paper, ruler, colored pencils.

Measuring the crown

1 Using the compass, walk away from the tree toward the north. Ask a friend to call out when you reach the edge of the crown. Place a marker at this point.

2 Repeat for the other seven main compass directions. Measure the distances back to the trunk with a tape measure and note them down.

3 Plot your results on graph paper. Measure 1 inch on the paper for each yard on the ground.

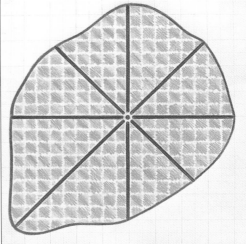

4 When you have sketched and colored in the crown's shape, count the squares and half squares to find its area. Do not count partial squares if they are less than a half.

ROOTS

WHEN you look at a tree, you can only see a part of it. Up to one-third lies hidden below ground. Unseen roots spread out underground as wide as the branches above. These roots anchor a tree in the ground and hold it up against the force of the wind. Main roots are thick and woody, like a tree's branches. They divide toward their ends into smaller and smaller roots. The smallest roots are covered with tiny hairs that have thin skins. These root hairs take up water and nutrients from the soil that are passed to larger roots and up through the trunk to the leaves. Nutrients help the tree grow strong and healthy.

Gale-force winds have snapped off this beech tree's main roots and blown it over. You can see some of the shallow roots that grew near the surface of the ground.

Shallow roots
Trees grow shallow roots where the soil is poor. All the nutrients lie in a thin, top layer of the soil.

Deeper roots
Trees grow deeper roots in rich soil. Most of the roots, however, still grow in a wide area near the surface.

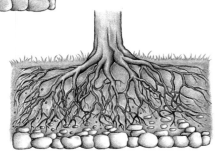

The banyan tree of India grows roots to support its spreading branches. Pillar roots grow down from the lower branches and take root in the ground. This helps the tree spread out over a wide area.

Many giant rainforest trees are over 500 feet tall, but their roots grow near the surface. To guard against toppling over, they also have wedge-shaped buttress roots growing up the sides of their trunks.

Mangrove trees grow in soft river mud. They support their long slender trunks with prop roots growing out of the trunk. Prop roots work like a tent's ropes, anchoring the tree in the mud.

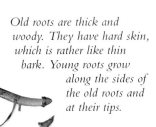

Old roots are thick and woody. They have hard skin, which is rather like thin bark. Young roots grow along the sides of the old roots and at their tips.

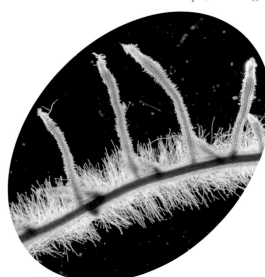

Just above its tip, a new root is covered in thousands of tiny root hairs. The hairs absorb water and nutrients from the soil around them.

PUMPING WATER

A̱ LL trees draw water from deep beneath the ground right up into their leaves, acting like a natural pump. Many trees are over 150 feet tall and pump hundreds of gallons of water a day. You can suck a drink up through a straw, but trees cannot use this method. Instead, they use a method called osmosis to force water upward. Osmosis works because there is a difference between the sap, or juice, inside the roots and the water in the ground outside. Sap contains large amounts of sugary substances. Ground water contains only tiny amounts of dissolved nutrients. We say that sap is more concentrated than ground water. Osmosis forces water from the soil (where concentration is low) through minute holes in the root skin to inside the root (where concentration is high). Tough-walled tubes carry the water up the trunk and into the leaves. The water evaporates from the leaves through tiny holes. As it evaporates, more water moves up to take its place.

To find out how difficult it is to suck up water, carefully join straws with tape. The longer the straw, the more difficult it is for you to suck up the drink. The best mechanical pumps can manage only 32 feet.

MATERIALS

You will need: large potato, cutting board, peeler, knife, teaspoon, 2 shallow dishes, water, sugar.

How osmosis works

1 You will need a large, smooth potato about 4 inches long and 2 inches across. Carefully peel the potato using a cutting board to protect your work surface.

2 Cut the peeled potato in half and then slice off the rounded ends. You will now have two round potato slices. Each slice should be about 1 inch thick.

You will need: stalk of celery with its leaves, clear beaker, water, food coloring.

How water travels up a stem

Trees and other plants move water upward through tubes called xylem vessels. You can easily see these tubes in celery. Cut ½ inch from the end of a stalk of celery. Put the celery into a beaker of colored water and let sit for one day.

Xylem vessel

You can see the colored water in the xylem tubes of the celery. Cut across the bottom of the stem for a better view.

3 Use a teaspoon to scoop out a hollow in each potato slice. Place each slice in its own shallow dish and fill the dishes with water to about ½ inch depth.

4 Half fill both hollows with water. Add ½ teaspoon of sugar to one hollow. Cover and let sit for one day. *(Dye has been added to the water here to make it visible.)*

5 The level of liquid in the sugary hollow has risen. Osmosis has made more water move into this potato from the dish. The level in the other potato has not risen.

TRUNKS AND BARK

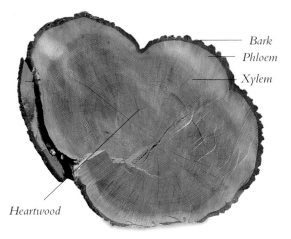

Bark
Phloem
Xylem
Heartwood

Bark protects the living, inner part of the tree. The phloem, or inner bark, carries food. The xylem, or inner wood, carries water from the roots to the leaves. The central part of the trunk is dead heartwood.

ARK is the woody skin that covers a tree. It prevents the tree from drying out and also helps protect against attack by animals and fungi. Bark can be thin and smooth or thick and knobbly, depending on the type of tree and its age. Young trees have smooth bark on their trunks and branches. Old bark stretches and cracks or peels as a tree grows fatter each year. Just underneath the bark is a delicate layer called the phloem. Trees make their own food that travels around in the phloem. If bark is damaged all around a tree trunk, the flow of food stops and the tree dies.

How bark ages

The bark of a young eucalyptus tree *(left)* is smooth and thin. As the tree grows, more and more layers of bark build up underneath. The bark of an old eucalyptus tree *(right)* is deeply cracked and wrinkled. Old layers of bark on the outside split as new layers on the inside push outward.

Under attack
Deer and other woodland animals chew bark when other food is scarce. Harmful insects or fungi can then enter through the wound, causing disease and more damage to the tree.

Insects and larvae
Stag beetles and other insects lay their eggs under the bark. The eggs hatch into soft-bodied grubs, which eat deeper into the wood with their powerful jaws.

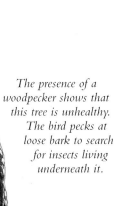

The presence of a woodpecker shows that this tree is unhealthy. The bird pecks at loose bark to search for insects living underneath it.

This ancient willow tree is hollow because the dead heartwood has rotted away. Firm bark still protects the phloem and the xylem layers, so the tree continues to live and grow.

LOOKING AT BARK

You will need: magnifying glass, field guide, notebook, pencil, binoculars.

DIFFERENT trees have different sorts of bark. A massive beech tree has smooth, thin bark that is about ½ inch deep. A redwood tree of the same size has hairy, fibrous bark that is up to 6 inches thick. Many conifers, such as pines and spruces, have bark that flakes off in small pieces. The appearance of the bark can help you decide what species, or type, a tree is. It can also tell you how old a tree is – young trees have smooth, thin bark that cracks and wrinkles as the tree matures. If you look closely at the bark you can discover many clues about its life. For example, clinging to the surface there may be plants and fungi, both large and small. Hiding inside cracks and holes might be many different sorts of insects and other tiny creatures. Choose a tree and identify it using a field guide. Then, see what you can find out about your tree by becoming a bark detective!

Become a bark detective

1 Bark does not stretch but cracks and peels as a tree grows. Use a magnifying glass to search in the cracks during spring and summer for tiny insects and other creatures.

2 If you look under loose bark on rotten wood you may find white threads, called hyphae. These are part of a fungus and they are slowly digesting the dead wood.

3 The bark has fallen away from this dead tree revealing the holes chewed by beetle grubs underneath. Some grubs live under the bark for several years.

Bark rubbing
Make a collection of bark patterns to take home. Ask a friend to hold a sheet of paper steady against the bark. Rub the side of a crayon over the paper with long even strokes. Write the name of the tree beside each rubbing.

You will need: paper, crayon.

Horse chestnut

Red oak

You could make a special book to display your rubbings. Punch holes into pieces of colored cardboard and link them together with ribbon. Stick your rubbings onto each page. You could include a silhouette of each tree as well. Remember to label each page with the name of the tree.

4 Where the bark is damp, you will often find powdery green patches. These are millions of microscopic plants called algae that live side by side on the bark's surface.

5 Look at the upper branches with binoculars. You may find signs of squirrels and other animals. They strip away soft bark, often causing branches to die and drop off.

NEEDLES AND LEAVES

WHICH species, or types, of trees grow near your home? Are they oaks, maples, eucalyptus, acacias or pines? There are thousands of different species, but most belong to just two main groups – coniferous, or conifer trees, and broad-leaved trees. Conifers, such as pines, firs and spruces, have needlelike leaves. They grow their seeds inside cones, not flowers. Most conifers are evergreen and are covered with leaves all year round. Broad-leaved trees, such as oaks, birches and maples, have broad, flat leaves. In tropical climates, most broad-leaved trees are evergreen and grow new leaves steadily as older ones fall away. In colder climates, most broad-leaved trees are deciduous and lose all their leaves in the fall. Broad-leaved trees have flowers and grow their seeds inside fruits, such as nuts and berries.

Conifers, such as pines and spruces, are decorated as Christmas trees, a tradition that spread from Germany. Originally, their evergreen branches were seen as a symbol of hope for new life in the spring.

Evergreen holly
Holly is a broad-leaved evergreen tree. Its leaves are thick, so they are not damaged by freezing winter weather. A waxy coat prevents the leaves drying out when water is scarce.

You can see the light shining through this maple leaf. The leaves of deciduous broad-leaved trees are usually much thinner than evergreen leaves.

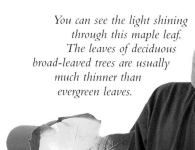

The seasons

Young leaf

Spring
The warmth of spring makes the rolled-up leaves of these birch trees burst from their buds. The leaves will grow quickly.

Mature leaf

Summer
In summer, the birch has a dense canopy of mature leaves, which catch the sunlight for photosynthesis.

Dying leaf

Fall
In the fall, all the food flows from the leaves into stems and roots. The leaves turn yellow and fall to the ground.

Winter
All through the cold and dark winter months, deciduous trees are like hibernating animals. Sap hardly moves at all and growth stops. The tree is waiting for the arrival of spring.

FROM BUD TO LEAF

L OOK closely at trees in winter, and you will see that they are not completely bare. Each twig has buds along its sides and at the tip. Buds have protective skins with tiny immature leaves and stems curled up inside. When spring sunshine warms the trees, buds begin to grow and swell. Finally they burst open, and small leaves emerge. Leaves contain pipes called veins. Water pumps into these veins, making the leaves stiffen and flatten as they grow to full size. To help identify trees, you can make a labeled collection of dried leaves. You can also make rubbings from leaves in the same way as bark rubbings.

Folded leaf

Bud scale

Short stem

This bud is almost ready to burst open. The tough bud scales protect the curled-up leaves inside.

Looking at branches
Gales sometimes rip young branches from trees. If you find one, place it in water and study the branch. You will find that it has buds and leaves at different stages of development.

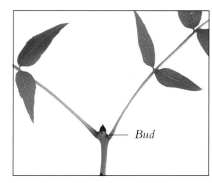

Bud

At the top of this ash twig, between two leaves, there is an unopened bud. It contains tiny leaves and a shoot that will grow in spring and make the twig longer.

You will need: gloves, leaves, paper towels, heavy books, notebook, glue, pencil, field guide.

Leaf pressings

1 To start your leaf collection, you can pick up fallen leaves or cut fresh ones. Wear gloves to protect your hands and make sure you have permission to cut fresh leaves.

2 To dry and flatten your leaves, place sheets of paper towels between the pages of a large and heavy book. Lay your leaves out on the paper on one side only.

3 When you have laid out all your leaves, close the books up and pile them on top of each other. Put more books on top. Make sure the pile cannot topple over and will not get disturbed. The weight presses the leaves flat while the paper towels absorb moisture.

4 Wait for at least one month until the leaves are flat and dry. Glue them into your notebook or onto sheets of thick paper and make them into a book. Use a field guide to identify each leaf.

Pressed leaves keep their shape and can last forever, if they are kept dry.

LIVING PROCESSES

JUST like you, trees are living things. You have to eat to stay alive and grow, but trees and other plants do not have to take in food. They make their own, using water from the ground and carbon dioxide gas from the air. Leaves contain a green substance called chlorophyll, that traps the energy from sunlight. The trapped energy joins water and carbon dioxide to make oxygen and sugary glucose. This whole process is called photosynthesis. Trees use glucose to make new materials and supply energy for growth. The oxygen escapes back into the air and makes it good for us to breathe.

Trees spread their leaves as wide as possible to absorb as much energy as they can from sunlight. They use the energy to make sugary glucose.

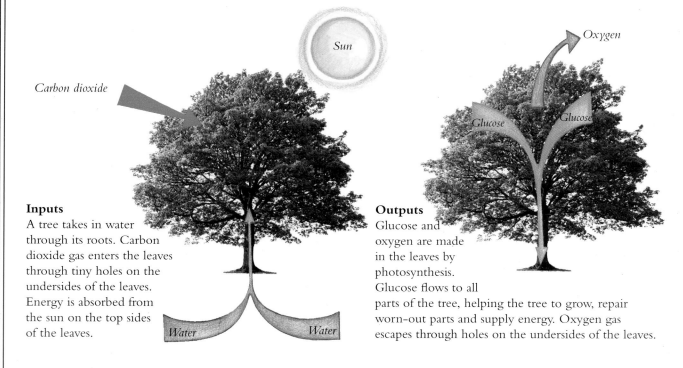

Sun

Carbon dioxide

Oxygen

Glucose *Glucose*

Water *Water*

Inputs
A tree takes in water through its roots. Carbon dioxide gas enters the leaves through tiny holes on the undersides of the leaves. Energy is absorbed from the sun on the top sides of the leaves.

Outputs
Glucose and oxygen are made in the leaves by photosynthesis. Glucose flows to all parts of the tree, helping the tree to grow, repair worn-out parts and supply energy. Oxygen gas escapes through holes on the undersides of the leaves.

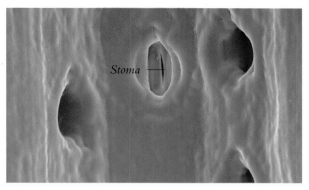

Stomata
Gases flow in and out of leaves through microscopic holes called stomata (one hole is called a stoma). The stomata shown here have been magnified about 200 times so you can see them.

Stoma

Vein

Veins
Liquids flow in
and out of leaves
through pipes called veins. On the underside of a leaf, you can see that the veins also act like ribs that help to stiffen the leaf and keep it flat.

Photosynthesis
Photosynthesis happens near the top surface of a leaf where sunlight is strongest.

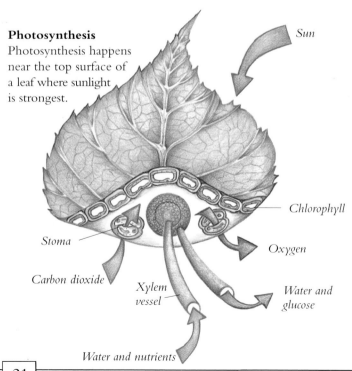

Sun

Chlorophyll

Stoma

Oxygen

Carbon dioxide

Xylem vessel

Water and glucose

Water and nutrients

FACT BOX
• If photosynthesis stopped, so would all life on earth. Photosynthesis is the ultimate source of all food on earth, because all animals either eat plants or eat other animals that live on plants. The oxygen it releases is the source of all oxygen in our atmosphere.

• The skin around a leaf cell is less than one-thousandth of an inch thick.

• Breathing air and burning fuel use up oxygen and produce carbon dioxide. Four large trees take all day to replace the oxygen used by a car driven for one hour.

LIGHT AND WATER

Trees must have light to live. Without light, they cannot use photosynthesis to make their own food. Look at a leaf and you will see that the top side is usually greener than the underside. This is because there is more chlorophyll here where the light is strongest. In shady forests, young trees race each other to reach the light above. They change direction as they grow, avoiding obstacles that block the light.

Warm sunshine also makes water evaporate from leaves, in the same way that wet clothes dry on the clothesline. Water moves up from the roots and into the leaves. Here it is changed from a liquid into an invisible gas called water vapor and escapes through holes in the leaves. This process is called transpiration.

These are trees in a tropical rain forest. They pass millions of gallons of water vapor into the air each day. The vapor forms thick clouds of tiny water droplets above the forest.

MATERIALS

You will need: clear plastic bag, yarn.

Transpiration at work

1 Find a tree with leaves you can easily reach. Choose some leaves at the end of a branch in a shady spot. Push the leaves inside the bag and tie the neck around the branch.

2 Next morning you should find droplets of water clouding the inside of the bag. The leaves have given off water vapor. The gas has cooled and reverted to liquid water.

Searching for the light

1 Watch a plant search for the light as it grows, by making a maze. Cut a hole in the end of a shoe box and stick eight flaps of cardboard inside with tape as shown here.

2 Paint the inside of the box and lid black. The black paint will stop the light, which is entering through the hole at one end, being reflected around inside the box.

3 Plant a bean in a small pot of compost. Water the soil each day to keep it moist but not wet. Some days water may not be necessary.

4 When the plant has a shoot, stand it in the bottom of your maze. Close the lid tightly and place the maze in a sunny spot. Once a day, remove the lid to see if the seedling needs watering.

The plant will find its way through the maze as it steadily moves toward the light. Eventually it will poke out through the hole at the top of the shoe box.

M A T E R I A L S

You will need: shoe box, scissors, stiff cardboard, tape, black paint, paintbrush, flowerpot, compost, runner bean, watering can, water.

POLLINATION

Wind pollination
Shake a hazel catkin, and it can scatter over 2 million pollen grains into the air. By chance, the wind may carry some away to the female flowers.

A LL trees grow from seeds. Even a mighty 250 feet high redwood starts life from a seed the size of your fingernail. There are two ways that trees make seeds – either inside cones or inside flowers. Cone-bearing trees include pines and firs. Flowering trees include oaks and maples. To make seeds, trees have male parts and female parts. In spring, the female parts contain tiny unripe seeds called ovules, while the male parts make grains of dustlike pollen. Pollen must join with ovules before they can grow into ripe seeds. The male and female parts may be on the same tree or on separate trees far apart from one another. The way pollen travels from the male parts to the female parts is called pollination.

Bird pollination
This Costa Rican hummingbird pollinates flowers with its long beak as it probes for nectar. Some flowers have special shapes, colors and nectar to attract particular sorts of animals such as bats and birds.

Insect pollination
While a bee feeds on the sugary nectar made by an apple flower, its body becomes coated in sticky pollen. As it moves to the next flower, it pollinates the female parts. Many trees use flowers to attract insects to spread their pollen.

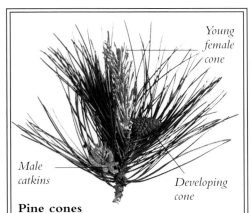

Young female cone

Male catkins

Developing cone

Pine cones

In early summer, pine trees grow tiny female cones containing ovules. Yellow catkins, or male cones, make pollen that they scatter into the air. Later, the male parts shrivel away, and the female cones start to swell and ripen.

How a cedar cone develops

In the fall, cedar trees grow tiny female cones containing ovules. After pollination, when the ovules are fertilized, the female cones start to swell and turn hard.

As the female cone matures, the scales become woody and change color from green to brown. Cones can take up to three years to mature.

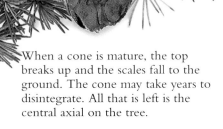

When a cone is mature, the top breaks up and the scales fall to the ground. The cone may take years to disintegrate. All that is left is the central axial on the tree.

The seeds are released as the scales fall. The seeds have papery wings to help them fly far away from the parent tree.

FROM FLOWER TO FRUIT

How many fruits can you think of that grow on trees? Obvious examples include apples, oranges, plums and pears. They have juicy flesh with seeds buried deep inside. The seeds grew from tiny ovules fertilized by pollen. Most of the fleshy part grew from the ovary wall that surrounded the ovules. Winged sycamore seeds, shiny chestnut conkers and hard walnuts grow in the same way. They are called fruits, too. Fruits grow on trees that use flowers to reproduce. The seeds are wrapped up inside a container, the fruit, that protects the developing seeds until they are ripe and ready to be spread by the wind or animals. Cones that grow on pines, firs and spruces are not fruits.

Each seed grows loose, because it is tucked between the scales of a cone.

Flowers, such as this elder blossom, are a specialized part of the plant. They develop into fruits and seeds.

Flowers, fruits and seeds

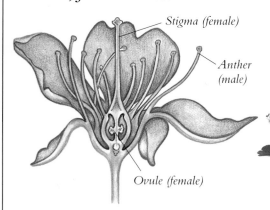

Stigma (female)

Anther (male)

Ovule (female)

Swollen ovary

Flower

This diagram shows a flower cut in half. Pollen is made by the anthers. When a pollen grain lands on the stigma, part of it grows down to the ovary and fertilizes the ovule.

After fertilization, the petals drop off. The ovary swells to form a fruit. Inside, the fertilized ovule becomes a seed. The seed contains a tiny plant called the embryo, as well as a store of food.

The fruit continues to swell and grow as the seed inside develops. When the seed is ready, the fruit ripens. The brightly colored succulent fruits are eaten by animals who spread the seeds.

Seed

Pit

Plums are a type of fruit called a drupe. They have juicy flesh and a single hard pit that contains the seed. Peaches and cherries are drupes, too.

Oranges are fleshy, brightly colored citrus fruits with a strong smell and many seeds. Lemons and limes are also citrus fruits.

Apple blossoms bloom in early spring. Apples have lots of seeds, called pips, inside a core. Some apples turn red as they ripen.

Seed

Seed

A walnut is a drupe, but on the tree it is covered by a tough green skin instead of juicy flesh. The seed is inside the hard, woody shell.

When you eat a fruit, such as a juicy apple, be sure to look out for the seeds.

FRUITS AND SEEDS

T HERE are many different kinds of fruits. Some fruits are soft, such as apples and oranges, and others are hard, such as acorns and walnuts. Even tough little hawthorn berries and sycamore wings are fruits. We call them fruits because they all have seeds protected inside a container. The container may be the soft flesh of a plum or the hard shell of a hazelnut. Hard or soft, small or large, all fruits contain seeds. You can try to find the seeds hidden inside different fruits. Some examples are given here. If you want to try others, it is safest to use edible fruits bought at your local store.

M A T E R I A L S

You will need: cutting board, sharp knife, tweezers, magnifying glass, apple, orange, apricot, plum, lemon, hazelnut, nutcracker, scissors.

Looking at apple seeds

1 Cut open an apple with a sharp knife. Inside, you will find several brown seeds, or pips, in the center. Use the tweezers to remove as many of the seeds as you want.

Apple seed

2 With tweezers, carefully remove the soft outer skin of a seed. Underneath the skin you will find a slippery white seed. Treat it carefully – it is very delicate.

3 Look under a magnifier to see the cotyledon and embryo (at tip). The cotyledon provides food for the embryo, which will grow into a new root and shoot.

Orange

Apricot

Plum

Lemon

Apple

Soft fruits

These fruits are soft, fleshy and sweet. Like most fruits, they have grown from the ovaries inside female flowers. Open any fruit and inside you will find seeds.

Looking inside a nut

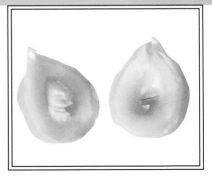

1 Nuts are fruits that have their seeds inside a hard container. Carefully crack open a hazelnut with a nutcracker and look for the seed (nut kernel) inside.

2 Use scissors to scrape off the dark outer skin from the kernel. You should then be able to separate the white hazelnut into two halves. Look at these with a magnifying glass.

3 Inside the nut is a tiny embryo. This part grows into roots and a stem. The two larger parts are the cotyledons, which supply energy for the sprouting seed to grow.

SCATTERING SEEDS

THE best place for many young animals to grow up is close to their parents. The adults protect their young and provide them with food and shelter. However, the best place for a young tree to grow up is as far away as possible from adult trees and from other seeds. Seeds that sprout beneath other trees will not grow strong and healthy. They are sheltered from the light and have to share precious water and nutrients. To give their offspring a good start in life, many trees disperse, or scatter, their seeds far and wide. There are many different ways of dispersing seeds, and the shape and design of a tree's fruit reflects these different methods.

Gyrocopter
You can make a model maple seed, or gyrocopter. Cut a strip of paper in half to about one-third its length. Bend the two ends back, as shown below, and attach a paper clip to the end. What happens when you let it fall?

Fruit

Gyrocopter

Winged seeds
Maple trees have winged fruits growing in pairs. One seed is attached to each wing.

When the seeds are ripe, the fruit falls from the tree. The wings spin like the blades of a helicopter, slowing it down and carrying it far away in a strong wind.

On the ground, the fruit dries out and splits into two.

Animal carriers
Animals such as this orangutan enjoy sweet fleshy fruits. They eat the flesh and then throw away the seeds, often far away from where they picked the fruit.

Bird carriers
Some seeds with hard coats pass unchanged through fruit-eating birds and bats. They can finally emerge many miles away. The seeds land on the ground wrapped in a package full of nutrients!

Carried by water
Coconuts float on water. They grow on palm trees that drop their fruits into rivers or the sea. Some young palms sprout thousands of miles away from where they started.

You will find some trees growing in very strange places. This pine tree may have grown from a seed that was carried in the wind or dropped by a bird.

31

GERMINATION

You will need: gloves, 5 inch (diameter) flowerpot, compost, acorns or another tree's seeds, trowel, watering can.

WHEN a seed begins to grow, we say that it has germinated. Germination starts when warmth and moisture swell the seed and split its skin. A tiny root grows downward and a thin shoot pushes up toward the light. The root and the shoot have grown from the smallest part of the seed, called the embryo. Food energy for growth comes from the largest parts, which are called the cotyledons. This project will show you how to germinate a seed and help it grow into a tree. You can also germinate beans in a glass jar and see that whichever way up you place the seed, the root will grow down and the shoot will grow up.

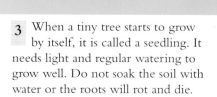

Germinate an acorn

1 Fill the flowerpot with compost and bury an acorn just beneath the surface. Put in a warm place and keep the soil moist. Plant several acorns, as one may not germinate.

2 This acorn has germinated. The brown root has started to grow downward into the soil and the green shoot has started to grow toward the light.

3 When a tiny tree starts to grow by itself, it is called a seedling. It needs light and regular watering to grow well. Do not soak the soil with water or the roots will rot and die.

4 Your seedling should grow rapidly for a few weeks and then stop. During winter it will need very little water. Next spring you can remove the seedling from its pot and plant it outside. Choose a good spot with an adult. Be careful not to disturb the roots when you do this.

5 This young oak tree is called a sapling and is about ten years old. You and your friends may have grown tree seedlings and planted them at your school. You do not have to grow your trees from seed. You can save time by buying seedlings at tree nurseries. Germinating a seed takes about two months.

You will need: glass jar, blotting paper or newspaper, fava bean or runner bean seed, water.

How a seed grows

1 Curl blotting paper inside a jar. Push a bean seed halfway down between the paper and the glass. Add water to a depth of 1 inch and stand the jar in a light, warm place.

2 When the seed germinates, you can see the root growing downward. Turn the jar so that the root points to the right. What do you think will happen?

The root has changed direction so it is growing downward again.

CONIFER FORESTS

Forests of conifers grow in a band across northern North America, Europe and Asia.

DIFFERENT kinds of trees grow naturally in different parts of the world. Where they grow depends mainly on the climate. Evergreen conifer trees, such as pines and firs, usually grow where the climate is cold. Long snowy winters are followed by short cool summers with moderate amounts of rain. The trees often grow close together, shutting out the light and making it difficult for some plants to grow there too. A forest is a community of many different plants and animals all living together. All these living things depend on each other, and it takes many centuries for a natural forest to grow.

Growth of a forest

Forests spread very slowly in a series of steps called a succession. Thousands of years ago, simple plants such as lichens and mosses lived on bare rock. Shallow soil gradually formed as they lived and died, then rotted away.

Grasses and small plants, such as arctic willow, then covered the ground. Centuries of growth, death and decomposition steadily made the soil deeper. Conditions became suitable for shrubs, such as heather, and small trees to grow.

Eventually the soil became deep enough to support trees. Young conifers started to grow. Their fallen leaves rotted slowly making the soil acidic. Ferns sprang up in the gaps between the trees. If left alone, this would have developed into a forest.

In a conifer forest
Hemlocks, cypresses and giant redwoods grow in the North American forests. Woodpeckers and chipmunks search for insects and seeds in the trees. Ferns grow on the gloomy forest floor. Moose and beavers live in lakes, and black bears scavenge for food to eat.

Needles and scales
All conifers have either needlelike leaves or scalelike leaves. Sitka spruce trees have needle-shaped leaves that grow in clusters. Cypress trees have needlelike young leaves and flattened, scalelike adult leaves.

Redwood

Pine

Sitka spruce

Cypress

TEMPERATE FORESTS

Large temperate forests are found in North America, Europe, Asia and Australia.

BROAD-LEAVED, deciduous trees, such as oak, ash and maple, grow in temperate climates, away from the hot dry tropics or the snowy lands of the arctic. The weather is warm and moist, with warm wet summers followed by short cold winters. A natural deciduous forest in summer is full of life. There are many more kinds of trees than in a northern coniferous forest. Sunlight pours down through gaps in the canopy, helping flowers, grasses and bushes to grow. All these plants provide food and shelter for a huge variety of creatures.

Simple leaves
Broad-leaved trees have either simple leaves or compound leaves. These three leaves are all simple leaves. Each leaf grows in one piece at the end of its own stalk.

Oak

Common beech

Poplar

In a temperate forest
Beech, ash and oak grow in this European forest. Squirrels and birds live in the trees. Bluebells, wood anemones and badgers live on the forest floor. Worms and moles burrow underground. Larger animals include deer, and there may even be wild pigs and brown bears.

Compound leaves
Compound leaves are made up of several small leaflets joined to a single stalk. The leaflets may be arranged along each side of the stalk, or they may all be attached to one point.

Laburnum

Horse chestnut

False acacia

LIFE IN A TREE

Have you ever walked through a forest in summer? You most probably saw hundreds of trees, but did not notice the thousands of animals living in them. Woodland creatures are usually very secretive. Small animals are caught and eaten if they do not hide carefully. Larger animals scare away their food if they are noisy. You may not spot the animals themselves, but you can often find the clues they leave behind. Why not spend an afternoon with some friends being nature detectives? The best place to visit is mixed woodland where there are deciduous broad-leaved trees as well as evergreen conifers. Do not forget to take along an adult to carry the sandwiches and keep you safe.

You will need: magnifying glass, field guide, large sheet of paper or cloth, paintbrush, jars and boxes, notebook, pencil.

Become a nature detective

1 On the ground, you may find signs of feeding. These include gnawed pine cones and half-eaten nuts and fruits. A field guide will suggest the animals responsible.

2 Look for round holes in dead or dying trees. A woodpecker makes its nest by chipping its way into a hollow tree. Later on, the nest is often used by other birds or animals.

3 This tree is dead and is losing its bark. The wood is soft because it is rotting. Birds and small animals dig holes in the trunk as they search for insects to eat.

Creature hunt

1 See how many insects you can find living up a tree. You do not have to climb up – simply spread a large sheet of paper or a cloth under a low leafy branch.

2 Shake the branch with short quick movements. Insects and other small creatures will fall onto your sheet.

3 Before they can scurry away, use your paintbrush to sweep each creature into a clear jar.

4 What have you caught? A magnifying glass will help you make drawings in your notebook. Use a field guide to identify each creature.

5 When you have finished, release your captives near the foot of the tree where you found them. They will crawl back up the trunk and carry on with their lives.

TROPICAL TREES

TROPICAL countries lie close to the equator. The weather is hot, and daylight lasts for 12 hours for most of the year. Rain forests grow in tropical regions where heavy rain falls almost continuously. Trees and other plants grow all year round to make a dense jungle that is bursting with life. Some other tropical countries have very little rainfall. The sun beats down on barren soil that is dry and sandy. Only a few palms and other specially adapted trees can grow well. They store water in their trunks and roots, and they have long thin leaves that lose water very slowly.

Tropical rain forests grow in South America, Africa, Asia and Australia.

Drip-tip leaves
Many rain forest trees have deeply grooved leaves with downward pointing drip-tips at their ends. These quickly drain rainwater away and prevent leaves from sagging on stalks.

Rainforest canopy
The trees grow tightly packed together in this rain forest in Cameroon, Central Africa. Seen from the air, the treetops join to make a dense layer called the canopy. The canopy layer is between 100 and 150 feet above the ground.

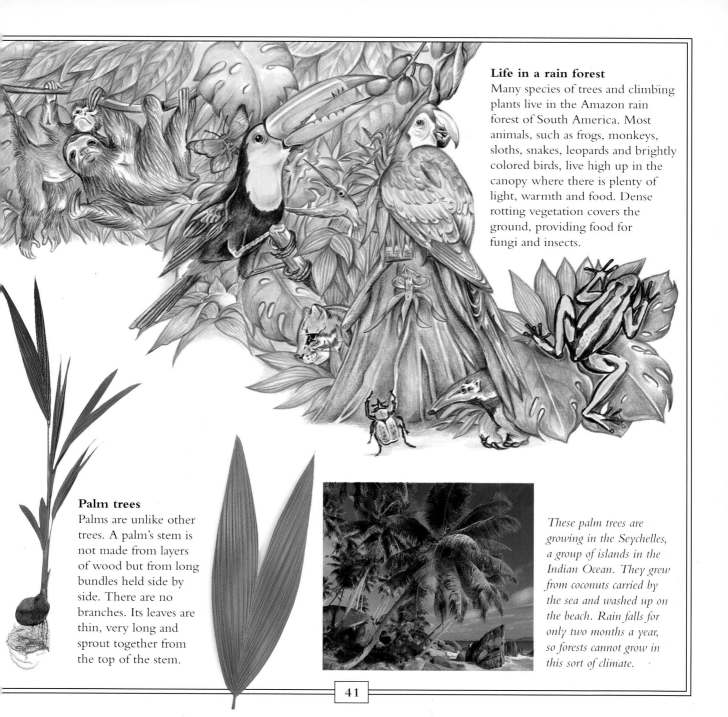

Life in a rain forest

Many species of trees and climbing plants live in the Amazon rain forest of South America. Most animals, such as frogs, monkeys, sloths, snakes, leopards and brightly colored birds, live high up in the canopy where there is plenty of light, warmth and food. Dense rotting vegetation covers the ground, providing food for fungi and insects.

Palm trees

Palms are unlike other trees. A palm's stem is not made from layers of wood but from long bundles held side by side. There are no branches. Its leaves are thin, very long and sprout together from the top of the stem.

These palm trees are growing in the Seychelles, a group of islands in the Indian Ocean. They grew from coconuts carried by the sea and washed up on the beach. Rain falls for only two months a year, so forests cannot grow in this sort of climate.

SAVANNA WOODLAND

SAVANNA is a dry, tropical area. For as far as you can see, the ground is covered with an endless layer of dry grass. There are occasional low shrubs and bushes. Trees grow alone or in widely spaced small groups. Forests cannot grow because the dry season lasts for most of the year. The trees that do grow here are species that can survive for a long time without water. Rain falls for two or three months when seeds germinate, the grass turns green and flowers bloom. Trees and other plants store water in their roots and stems to last them through the dry months to come.

Tropical grasslands are found in South America, Africa, Asia and Australia.

Drought defences

Euphorbia trees have small leaves to help cut down on water loss due to evaporation. They also have an unpleasant tasting sap that helps to protect the plant from being eaten by hungry animals.

Koalas

Koalas live in dry savanna woodlands in eastern Australia. They live on a constant diet of eucalyptus leaves. These trees originally came from Australia, but are now planted worldwide. They grow very fast, even in dry conditions.

Life on the savanna

The African savanna is dotted with drought resistant trees, such as baobabs, or bottle trees, and acacias. Herds of zebra, antelope and gazelles feed on the grass, while taller giraffes and elephants can reach up into the trees and strip the branches of their leaves. Dung beetles clear up the animal droppings, while vultures look out for a carcass left by a lion and lizards search for insects.

Thorn trees

Acacias are very common on the African savanna. They are also called thorn trees because of the sharp spines that grow among the leaves. Despite their prickles, many animals rely on acacia leaves for food. Acacias bloom in the wet season.

Storing water

Baobabs have roots that spread out over a wide area. During the rainy season the trees collect water and store it in their spongy trunks. The distance around a baobab's trunk can be almost as much as its height.

SWAMPS

Mangroves growing at the estuary of a river in Australia. Their roots are revealed at low tide.

SWAMPS are places where the ground is permanently waterlogged. The muddy ground is covered with a layer of water for much of the time. There are two sorts of swamps – freshwater and saltwater. Freshwater swamps are found in flat low-lying places. Water from streams and rain flows away very slowly. Saltwater swamps are found in muddy river estuaries close to the sea. The tide flows in and out twice a day, drowning the flat river banks with sea water. Most trees cannot survive in swamps because they need fresh water and air around their roots. Some swamps are full of trees that use special methods to survive.

FACT BOX

• The only trees that can grow in salty water are some types of mangroves. Their seeds start to grow while they are still attached to the tree. When the seeds drop into the mud, they quickly put down roots so they are not washed away by the tide.

• A freshwater swamp is formed from a shallow lake surrounded by plants. As leaves and flowers fall into the water, a layer of ooze builds up. The ooze slowly accumulates to form a swamp.

• The world's largest swamp is the Gran Pantanal in Brazil. It covers an area that is about the same size as the state of Tennessee.

Swamp cypress
The swamp cypress grows in the freshwater swamps of the Southern states. It has spongy breathing roots that stick up above the waterlogged ground. Air enters the roots and spreads to the parts below the surface.

Life in a swamp

The swirling, muddy water of a mangrove swamp is home to kingfishers, giant water bugs, turtles, crocodiles and mud skippers.

Support roots

The *Rhizophora* mangrove tree supports itself on prop roots that absorb oxygen from the air. Unwanted salt from sea water is taken in through its roots and stored in special leaves that fall off when they are full.

Breathing roots

The *Avicennia* mangrove has breathing roots that grow upward. Their tips are above the surface when muddy water covers the main roots.

AMAZING TREES

This miniature tree is fully grown. It is the result of the Japanese art of tree pruning, called bonsai. Over many years, its roots and shoots have been carefully cut to limit its growth.

Have you ever come across any strange or peculiar looking trees? Some trees may look strange, but they need to be this way in order to survive. For example, a baobab tree uses its bloated trunk to store water for the dry season. Other trees are amazing because of their size. Trees grow throughout their lives, so a very old tree can be a very big tree. Some of the oldest and most massive living trees are the redwood trees of California that can grow to over 300 feet high. Trees grow outward as well as upward – a banyan tree in India has spread to almost a quarter mile across.

Fossilized trees

These tree trunks were alive millions of years ago. They sank into the ground and were slowly changed into stony fossils. Wind and rain uncovered them and they now lie on the surface of the Algerian desert in North Africa.

Giant redwoods

Californian redwood trees (*left*) take over 2,000 years to grow 300 feet high and can weigh over 6,000 tons. Their enormous size is shown by these nine-year-olds standing beside a typical Californian redwood trunk (*right*).

FACT BOX

• A giant wellingtonia, a type of redwood, weighs as much as 100 railroad locomotives.

• A fig tree in Calcutta Botanic Gardens, India, has a canopy 400 feet across. It almost covers the area of two football fields.

• The largest seeds are coco-de-mer treenuts, which can weigh over 500 pounds each.

• A wild fig tree at Echo Caves in South Africa has roots 350 feet deep.

Sack-of-potatoes tree

The very strange sack-of-potatoes tree has rounded dents in its trunk that make it look like a belly dancer's tummy. It is also called the desert rose because it blooms with pink flowers in winter. Its swollen trunk stores water.

Cucumber tree

The amazing cucumber tree also stores water in its thick trunk. It can survive extreme droughts by shedding all its leaves. The tree then stays dormant and protected until rain arrives.

Traveler's palm

The traveler's palm can provide thirsty people with a drink. It grows in hot countries. If a hole is made at the bottom of the stalk, where the leaf joins the trunk, refreshing watery sap spurts out.

LEAF FALL, DEATH AND DECAY

As the fall comes, trees prepare for winter. Delicate leaves would be harmed by cold winter winds, so the trees take back their food and seal them off at the base. The leaves change color and fall to the ground. All these colorful leaves have died, but they are still vital for the life of the trees above. As they lie on the ground they start to rot. Tiny living creatures, called decomposers, use them for food. Decomposers include microscopic bacteria, fungi, insects and other tiny animals. They digest the leaves and break them down, releasing nutrients the trees must have for growth in the coming spring. Life, death and decay are linked in an endless cycle.

A beech forest in the fall. The leaves dry out and turn golden yellow. Food and sap flow back into the trees, and the leaves fill with unwanted substances. The joints between the stalks and twigs loosen, and the leaves fall.

Decomposers

Dead leaves are food for decomposers such as wood lice. They eat the fallen leaves and pass many of the nutrients back into the soil, to be taken up again by the trees' roots.

Leaf skeleton

The thinnest part of a leaf is digested by decomposers first. The stalk, midrib and veins are the toughest parts. They form a skeleton that may take a year or more to be broken down.

The death of a tree
Toward the end of its life, a tree is invaded by decomposers, especially fungi. Fungi feed on the dead and living wood. Dead branches fall off as the wood is weakened. Finally, the trunk topples to the ground and rots away.

Leaves fall.

Nutrients dissolve in rain-water and sink into the soil.

Recycled life
Trees need nutrients from the soil to grow. These nutrients come from dead and rotting leaves, trees and animals. Fungi, microscopic bacteria and tiny animals break down the rotting material and recycle the nutrients back into the soil.

Dead leaves lie on the ground.

Tree rotters
About 15 years after this tree fell, its stump is steadily decaying. Tunneling insects have loosened the bark. Toadstools sprout from the tendrils of fungi that reach right through the stump as they digest the wood to a soggy pulp.

Fungi and animals decompose, or break down, the leaves.

LIFE IN THE LEAF LITTER

You will need: plastic soda bottles (large and small), scissors, plastic funnel, gloves, damp soil, sand, about 6 worms, damp rotting leaves, black paper.

I N the fall, piles of leaves litter the ground. Slowly they rot away, until it seems there is nothing left. Rotting does not happen by itself. The decomposers – millions of fungi, microscopic bacteria and tiny creatures – eat away at the leaves and break them down. Decomposers digest leaves and turn them into nutrients. These nutrients are important chemicals that dissolve in rainwater and trickle down to the tree roots below. Living trees need these recycled nutrients in order to grow. Earthworms work as decomposers. Make a wormery and you will see how worms pull dead leaves into their underground tunnels. You can also separate decomposers from the rotting leaves they live in with a lamp, a funnel and a jar.

Make a wormery

Worm burrowing

1 Cut the top off the large soda bottle, as shown. Place the smaller bottle inside the larger one. Make sure the gap is evenly spaced all the way around.

2 Fill the gap with layers of soil and sand to within 3 inches of the top. Press the soil down lightly. Gently place the worms on top of the soil and cover with dead leaves.

3 Cover with black paper. Keep the soil moist. After a few days, remove the paper to see how worms have tunneled away from the light and dragged leaves into their burrows.

Studying decomposers

You will need: plastic funnel, large clear jar, gloves, rotting leaves from a compost heap, damp tissue, black paper, desk lamp, magnifying glass, field guide.

1 Dead leaves are full of insects and other creatures. Separate them by using a lamp, a funnel and a jar. Put the funnel inside the jar, as shown.

2 Wearing gloves, loosely fill the funnel with dead leaves. Put damp tissue in the bottom of the jar. Wrap black paper around the jar to block out the light.

4 After an hour there will be several animals in the bottle. Look at them with a magnifying glass and use a field guide to identify them. When you have finished, return the animals to where you found them.

3 Place the lamp so that it shines onto the leaves. The animals will move away from the heat and light of the lamp and fall down the slippery funnel into the jar below.

PREHISTORIC TREES

This is the fossilized imprint of a leaf, 50 million years old. The leaf was buried in mud that turned to stone. Splitting open the stone shows where the leaf has left its mark.

OAK, eucalyptus, redwood and baobab – have these trees always grown on earth? Scientists think that trees were very different millions of years ago. Fossils dug up by palaeontologists, or scientists who study fossils, tell us that the earliest trees grew about 350 million years ago. This was long before the dinosaurs first lived on earth about 200 million years ago, or the first modern humans appeared just 1 million years ago. The earliest treelike plants looked a lot like bunches of feathery ferns growing at the top of a woody trunk. As time went by, these ancient trees gradually changed to suit the world as it changed. Trees that did not suit the environment became extinct, or died out. About 135 million years ago, the first trees with blossoms appeared on earth. Some trees today, such as the waxy-petaled magnolia, look very much like these early flowering trees.

How coal formed

Coal is called a fossil fuel. It was formed about 300 million years ago when many trees grew in steamy swamps. Dead trees fell into the stagnant muddy water. The water was too foul for decomposers to live in, so the wood did not rot away.

Soggy layers of vegetation – trees, leaves and other plants – all piled up on top of each other. Over millions of years, rivers dumped enormous amounts of mud and silt on top of them. The weight above compressed the vegetation into a solid mass.

Buried hundreds of yards below the surface, underground heat broke down the chemicals in the vegetation. Everything slowly fossilized and turned solid – trees and other vegetation became coal (the black layers) and the mud became layers of rock (as labeled).

Carboniferous period

About 350 to 280 million years ago was the Carboniferous period. Forests of giant ferns and trees like shaggy palms grew in vast swamps. Large amphibians and many insects thrived in the swamps.

Gingko leaves
One of the oldest surviving species of trees is the gingko, which first grew over 200 million years ago.

Cretaceous period

About 140 to 65 million years ago was the Cretaceous period. Many conifers were growing, and flowering deciduous trees appeared. Dinosaurs roamed across the land but died out by the end of this period.

Tertiary period

About 65 to 5 million years ago was the Tertiary period. Mammals quickly took over after the dinosaurs died out. Flowering deciduous trees became common.

WOOD AS A MATERIAL

How many things around you are made out of wood? There are tables and chairs and all sorts of furniture. Houses have wood floors held up by wood beams, and the roofs are supported by wooden rafters. Trees that have been cut down to make things are called timber. There are two kinds of timber – softwood and hardwood. Softwood comes from fast-growing conifers, such as pines and firs. Hardwood comes from slower-growing, broad-leaved trees, such as oak and maple. Planks are made by sawing tree trunks along their length. Larger sheets of plywood are made by shaving trunks into layers and gluing them together.

Many things are made out of wood, such as chairs and tables, paper, envelopes, books and pencils.

Chipboard is manufactured from sawdust and flakes of waste wood mixed with glue. Sheets of chipboard can be up to 7 feet wide, far wider than most tree trunks. It is used to make floors and cheap furniture.

Timber forests
This forester is cutting down a 60-year-old pine tree. The tree's side branches and thin tops will be cut away, leaving a long straight trunk. This will make it much easier to transport to the sawmill.

Sawmills
In the sawmill, machines rip off the bark and huge saws cut the trunk into planks. Timber must be seasoned, or dried out, before it can be used.

Carving wood

The main part of this Native American totem pole is made from a single tree trunk. Knives, axes and chisels are used to carve the wood into all sorts of different shapes and patterns.

Wood sailing ships

This is a reconstruction of the *Mayflower*, the ship that took the Pilgrim Fathers from England to North America in 1620. It took hundreds of trees to build a wood sailing ship. Oak trees were felled for the main hull, and pine trees were used for the deck planks.

Log rollers

About 4,500 years ago, the Egyptians built pyramids from huge blocks of stone. It is thought that they moved the blocks on wood sledges dragged along on rollers made of tree trunks.

CHEMICALS FROM TREES

Just like you and everything else in the universe, trees are made from chemicals. Trees take in simple chemicals from the ground and from the air. They use these substances and energy from the sun to make complicated chemicals. Many of these chemicals are useful to us. Some are found in the leaves, fruits or bark of particular trees. Many other chemicals are made by heating wood in huge ovens. The ovens are airtight so the wood does not burn. Heat boils the liquid chemicals out of the wood and changes them into gases. Cooling the gases makes a liquid mixture that can then be separated into different chemicals.

Rubber in car tires comes from trees. Sap called latex flows from cuts made in the bark of rubber trees. The latex is collected and processed to make rubber.

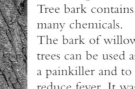

Eucalyptus leaves

Aspirin

Natural painkiller
Tree bark contains many chemicals. The bark of willow trees can be used as a painkiller and to reduce fever. It was the original source of the drug aspirin. Today, aspirin is made from chemicals found in crude oil.

Willow bark

Eucalyptus oil

Medicine leaves
Eucalyptus trees have oil in their leaves. The leaves are heated with steam to drive out the oil. It has a pleasant smell and is used to clear a stuffed-up nose that is blocked by a cold.

Turpentine

This artist is using oil paints. She is making them thinner and more runny by adding turpentine. This liquid is one of the main chemicals made by heating wood in an airtight oven.

Tanning hide

Animal skins are stiff until softened by a process called tanning. The skins are soaked in a mixture of bark chips and water. The chemicals in the bark help soften the skins.

FACT BOX

• Rosewood oil is used in perfumes, cosmetics and flavorings. It is steamed from the trunks of trees that grow in rain forests.

• Quinine is used to treat a deadly illness called malaria. It was first extracted from the bark of the South American cinchona tree.

• Gamboge is a brilliant yellow dye made from the sap of the Indian garcinia tree. It is used to dye the robes of Buddhist monks.

• Curare comes from the bark of a South American tree. Local people use it to tip their blowpipe darts. Doctors use it to relax the muscles of patients during operations.

• The sap of the Central American chicle tree is an ingredient of chewing gum.

• Sticky resin from pine trees is used to make medicine, glue, ink, perfume and insecticide.

Polished wood

You can make wood look more beautiful by polishing it regularly. Polish puts a protective layer on the surface. The waxes and resins used in polish come from the chemicals given off by heating wood.

POLLUTION AND DESTRUCTION

A tree damaged by acid rain. The acid rain strips the leaves of their protective coating of wax. The result is disease, usually followed by death.

EVERYTHING we do seems to have a hidden cost. Think of all the fuels we burn – coal to generate electricity, gas for cooking and heating, gas and diesel oil in cars and tunnels. Burning these fuels makes pollution. Two results of pollution are the greenhouse effect, which causes the earth to warm up, and acid rain, which poisons trees. We also like to eat hamburgers and end up destroying forests. Meat for hamburgers comes from cattle that eat grass. Ranchers in South America cut down rain forests to plant grass. One result is that heavy rain beats straight onto the ground and washes away the soil.

FACT BOX
• About 37 million acres of rain forest are cut down each year. This is about the size of the state of Florida.

• A total of 70 acres of forest is cleared every minute. It takes at least 150 years for forest to regrow on cleared land.

• Only 12 caoba trees are left in the wild, in the jungles of Ecuador, South America.

• Each year, fuels burnt in Great Britain pour about 6 million tons of acid gases into the air.

Acid rain
Polluting gases from power stations and vehicles rise into the air. The gases join with oxygen and water from the air and change into acid. The wind carries the pollution far from where it was made, to fall as acid rain on forests.

Destroying the rain forest

Every year, large areas of rain forest are cut down for timber. The ground is cleared by burning to make way for crops and grazing. Rain forest soil is very low in nutrients. Without the trees, it is soon exhausted and can only be farmed for a short time.

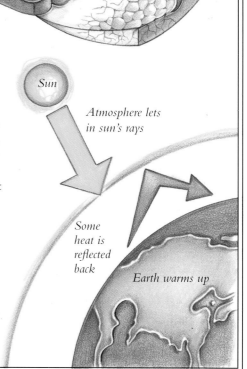

Deforestation

Tree roots help to hold the soil in place and leaves absorb the force of falling rain. When forests are cut down, soil is washed away. Rushing water causes flooding and exposed earth dries up.

Habitat loss

Many forest animals, like this sloth, are in danger of dying out as their habitat, or home, is cut down. They depend on the trees and plants for food and places to live.

Greenhouse effect

Burning fuels releases carbon dioxide gas into the atmosphere. Carbon dioxide lets the sun's rays through but traps some of the heat, much like the glass in a greenhouse. This effect is steadily making the earth's climate warmer.

Sun

Atmosphere lets in sun's rays

Some heat is reflected back

Earth warms up

CONSERVATION

How important do you think trees are? From reading this book, you should know that trees are very important. They change carbon dioxide gas in the air back into oxygen for us to breathe. They provide food, fuel, timber and chemicals for us to use. They keep the soil healthy and provide homes and food for countless other living things. Trees shade us from the sun and they are beautiful to look at all year round. We should take care of trees and make sure our woods and forests do not disappear. Humans have exploited trees for many years – we chop them down without thinking of the future. We should now do our best to conserve, or protect, trees and use them wisely. We need trees for the future, so we must get busy planning and planting them today.

If you have room in your garden or at school, why not replant your Christmas tree? Make sure to get a tree with good long roots and, when the festivities are over, dig a big hole and plant it outside.

Replanting
A specialized machine plants young fir seedlings in the ground. The young seedlings are grown in a nursery as stock for the replanting of forests. As forests are cut down for their timber, new trees will be planted for the future.

FACT BOX

• The world's oldest national park is Yellowstone in Wyoming, established in 1872. Banff National Park in Canada was set up in 1887, although coal mining and tree felling did not stop until 1923. More than 5 percent of the world's land is now protected.

• If you attend your first school for six years, there is just enough time for you to grow seedlings, plant a hedge and watch it grow to your own height before you leave.

• The United Nations Food and Agriculture Organization (FAO) was set up to teach people new ways of farming so they do not have to harm their land.

Forest fires
Bush fires in Australia destroy trees each year. Large forests have firebreaks, which are wide roadways with no trees. These help to stop fire from spreading.

Protected areas
This is Yellowstone National Park in Wyoming. Many countries have set aside woods and forests as conservation areas or national parks. Everything lives there with as little interference as possible from humans.

Coppice wood
Coppicing is a good way to make use of woodland resources. These shoots have grown from the stump of hazel trees. Every few years, the shoots are harvested and used for fuel or timber.

Recycling
Paper is made from wood chippings. One tree makes enough paper for only 400 copies of an ordinary newspaper. You can help conserve trees by saving old newspapers for recycling. Waste paper is mixed with wood chippings to make new paper.

MAKE A TREE MUSEUM

By now you should know a great deal about trees. Why not use your knowledge to make a tree museum for your friends to enjoy? You can collect leaves, bark, buds, cat-tails and flowers, as well as fruits, seeds and cones. You can also make rubbings of bark and leaves. Do not forget to look for things throughout the year – flowers and buds in spring, seeds and fruits in the fall. To complete your collection, you can cut pictures out of old magazines. Keep everything in shoe boxes until you can display it. Label your collection and note any interesting facts. Use pictures and drawings to make posters to hang on the wall.

When collecting items for your museum, make sure you have permission to take them away. Be thoughtful, tidy, methodical and safe. Always wear gloves when handling items.

Here is some of the equipment you might find useful to study trees and the creatures that live on them. Build up your stock of equipment along with your collection.

field guide

large glass jar

collecting pot

plastic boxes

plastic magnifier

paper

scissors

plastic bags

adhesive labels

magnifying glass

paintbrush

camera

colored pencils

gloves

pencil

notebook

Collecting specimens

1 How many different sorts of leaves can you find? Identify them using a field guide. Look at pages 18 and 19 for information to help you sort out and store your collection. Make sure you note the name of the tree each leaf comes from.

2 Only collect bark from dead trees that have fallen over. You can make bark rubbings of living trees. See page 15 for instructions on how to do this.

3 Springtime flowers soon wither and die. These young horse chestnuts will last much longer. Rather than picking flowers, it is better to take photos of them.

5 Start arranging your museum. You could make a display case from a shoe box by sticking in pieces of cardboard to make individual compartments. Work with friends to make a large display to help people learn about trees and how we must care for them.

4 You can look at young cones and leaves from the lowest branches of evergreen pines, firs and cedars. Look under these trees for cones that have fallen.

INDEX

acacia 16, 43
acid rain 58
acorn 5, 28, 32-3
aging 14
    measuring age 6
algae 15
    animal life 13-15, 35, 37-9, 41-3, 45
    decomposers 48-51
    land deforestation 59
    seed dispersal 31
anthers 26
apple 26-8
apricot 28
Archaeopteris 4
ash 18, 37
aspirin 56

bacteria 48-51
balsa 4
banyan 8, 46
baobab 43, 46, 52
bark 4-6, 12-15
bark rubbings 15
bats 24
beech 8, 14, 37, 48
bees 24
berries 16, 28-9
birch 16-17
birds 13, 24, 35, 37-9, 41, 43, 45
bird pollination 24
    seed dispersal 31
bonsai 46
bottle tree 43
branches 4-5
broad-leaved trees 16, 36-7, 54
bud scales 18
buds 4, 18

canopy 40
caoba 58
carbon dioxide 4,

20-1, 59-60
Carboniferous period 53
catkins 24-5
cedar 25
chemicals from trees 56-7
cherry 27
chewing gum 57
chicle 57
chlorophyll 20-3
Christmas tree 16, 60
cinchona 57
coal 52, 58
coco-de-mer 46
coconut 31, 41
cones 16, 24-6, 38
conifers 14, 16, 34-5, 54
conservation 60-1
coppicing 61
cotyledons 28-9, 32
Cretaceous period 53
crown 4
    measuring 7
cucumber tree 47
curare 57
cypress 35

dead trees 38, 49
deciduous trees 16, 36-7, 48-51
decomposers 48-51
deer 13
deforestation 58-9
desert rose 47
drip-tips 40
drought, defences against 42-3, 47
drupe 27

elder 26
embryo 26, 28-9, 32
eucalyptus 4, 12, 42, 56
euphorbia 42
evergreens 16, 34-5

fall 17, 48-51
false acacia 37
feeding and nutrients 4, 8-9, 12, 20-1, 48-51
fertilization 26
fig 46
fir 16, 24, 26, 54
flowers 4, 24-7, 63

forest fires 61
forests
    conifer 34-5
    deforestation 58-9
    rainforest 9, 40-1, 57-9
    temperate 36-7
    timber 54
fossils 46, 52-3
fruits 16, 26-31, 38
fungi 13-14, 41, 48-51

gamboge dye 57
garcinia 57
germination 32-3
gingko 53
glucose 20-1
Gran Pantanal 44
greenhouse effect 58-9
growth 4-5, 12
growth rings 6
gyrocopter 30

hardwood 54
hawthorn 28
hazel 24, 28-29
heartwood 12-13
height, measuring 7
holly 16
horse chestnut 26, 37
huon pine 4
hyphae 14

insect pollination 24
insects 13-14, 39, 41, 43, 48-9

koala 42

laburnum 37
leaf collection 18-19
leaf pressings 19
leaf rubbings 19
leaves 4-5, 16-19
    acid rain 58
    autumnal fall 48-51
    compound 36-37
    drip-tip 40
    needles 16, 35
    photosynthesis 20-2
    rotting 48-51
    scales 35
    simple 36

skeletons 48
stomata 21-2
transpiration 22-3
veins 18, 21
lemon 27-8
light 20-3
lime 27

magnolia 52
mangrove 9, 44-5
maple 16, 24, 30, 54
measuring a tree 6-7
museum, tree 62-3

needles 16, 35
nuts 16, 27-9, 38, 46

oak 4-5, 16, 24, 33, 36-7, 52, 54
orange 26-8
osmosis 10-11
ovaries 26
ovules 24, 26
oxygen 20-1, 60

palm 31, 40-1
paper recycling 61
peach 27
pear 26
petals 26
phloem 12-13
photosynthesis 20-2
pine 4, 16, 24-6, 31, 54, 57
plum 26-8
polish, wood 57
pollen 24, 26
pollination 24-6
pollution 58-9
poplar 36
prehistoric trees 4, 52-3

quinine 57

rainforest 9, 40-1, 57-9
redwood 14, 24, 35, 46, 52
resin 57
root hairs 8-9
roots 4-5, 8-9, 32-3
    buttress roots 9
    depth 8-9

pillar roots 8
prop roots 9, 45

spread 4, 8
swamp-growing plants 44-5
    rosewood 57
    rubber 56
sack-of-potatoes tree 47
salt water swamps 44-5
sap 4, 56-7
saplings 33
savanna woodland 42-3
scale-like leaves 35
seasons 17
seedlings 32-3
seeds 5, 16, 24-31, 46
    dispersal 30-1
    germination 32-3
shoots 18
sitka spruce 4, 35
softwood 54
spring 17
spruce 16, 26, 35
squirrel 15, 37
stigmas 26
stomata 21-22
succession 34
summer 17
sunlight 20-3
swamp cypress 44
swamps 9, 44-5
sycamore 26, 28

tanning 57
temperate forests 36-7
Tertiary period 53
thorn tree 43
thorns 43
timber 54-5
transpiration 22-3
traveler's palm 47
tropical regions
    rainforest 40-1
    savanna woodland 42-3
trunk 4-5, 12-13
turpentine 57
twigs 4-5, 18

veins 18, 21

walnut 26-8

water supply 10-12, 18, 20-3
willow 13, 56
wind pollination 24
winged seeds 26, 28, 30
winter 17
wood 54-7
woodlice 48
woodpecker 13, 35, 38
worms 50

xylem 12-13